ANCIENT EGYPTIAN DESIGN

ANCIENT EGYPTIAN DESIGN

DOVERPICTURA

DOVER PUBLICATIONS, INC. | Mineola, New York

Selected and designed by Luisa Gloria and Alan Weller.

Ancient Egyptian Design is a new work, first published by Dover Publications, Inc., in 2007.

The CD-ROM file names correspond to the images in the book. All of the artwork stored on the CD-ROM can be imported directly into a wide range of design and word-processing programs on either Windows or Macintosh platforms. No further installation is necessary.

ISBN-10: 0-486-99806-1
ISBN-13: 978-0-486-99806-0

Manufactured in the United States of America
Dover Publications, Inc., 31 East 2nd Street, Mineola, NY 11501
www.doverpublications.com

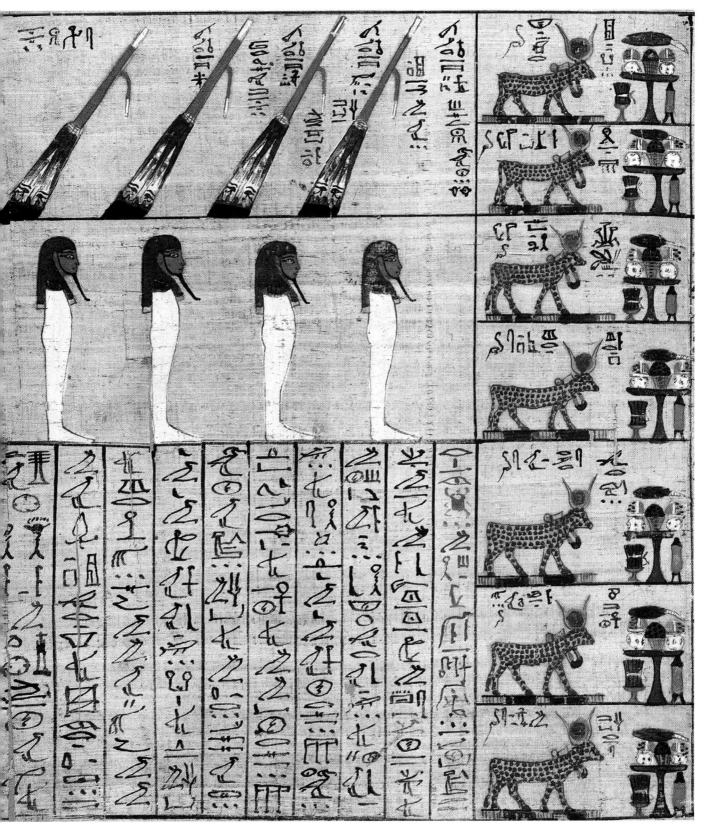

010

011
012
013
014
14

016

020 (background)

023

024 (background)

029

030

031

032

034

035

036-039

041

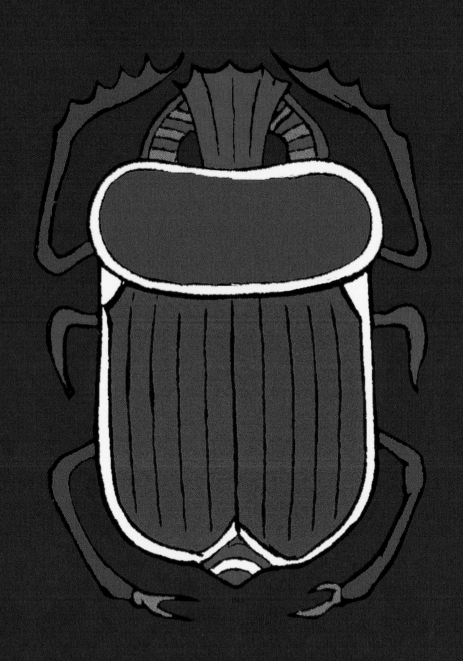

045

046 047 (ba

049

050 (background)

051

052

054

055 (background)

058

059

060

50

063

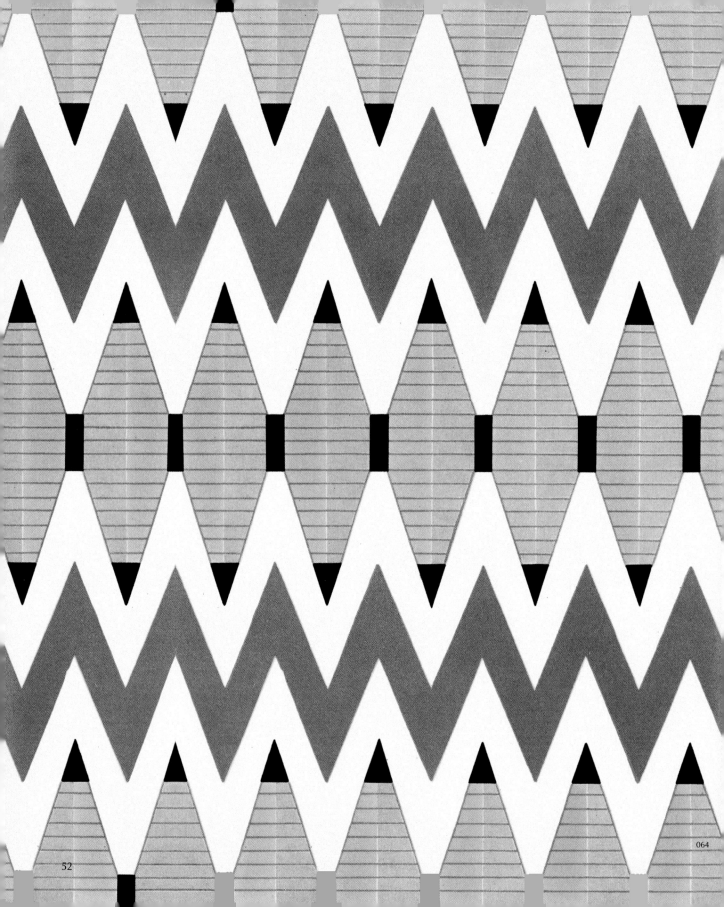

065

066

069

070

072

073

074

075

076

077

078

081

083

084

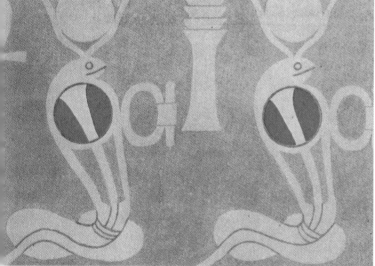

086

085

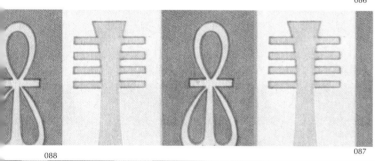

088

087

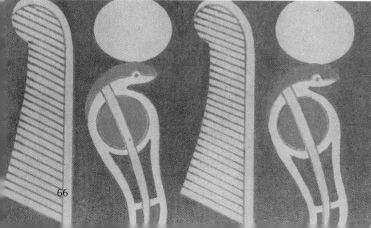

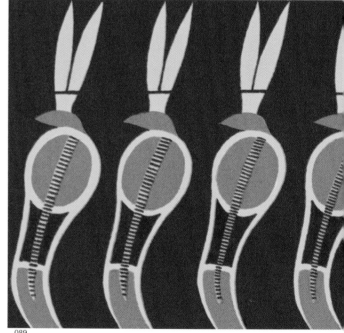

089

090

66

091

092

093 (background)

094

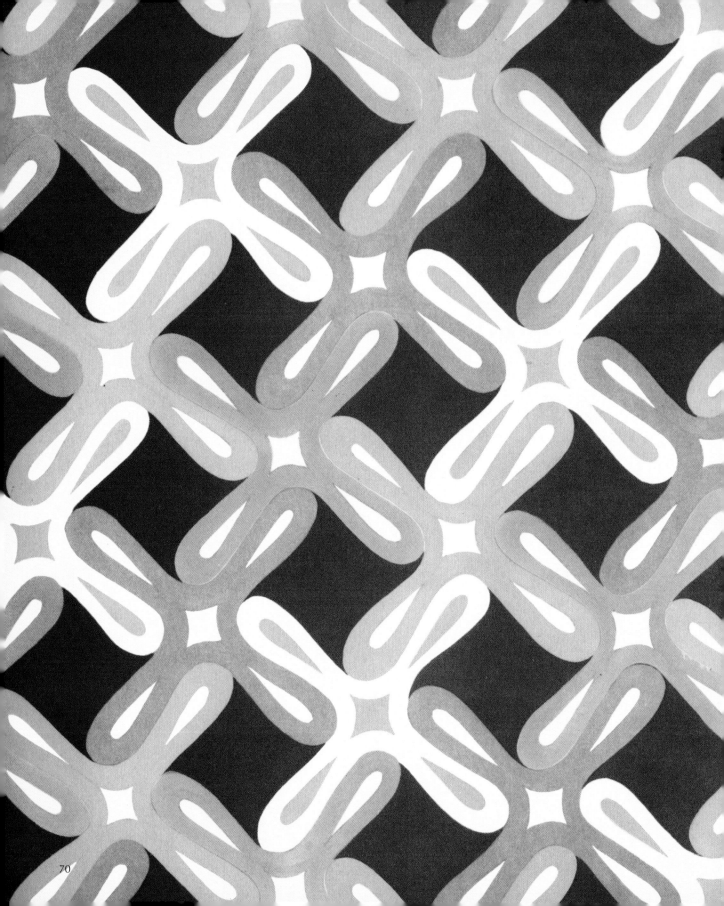

096

097

72

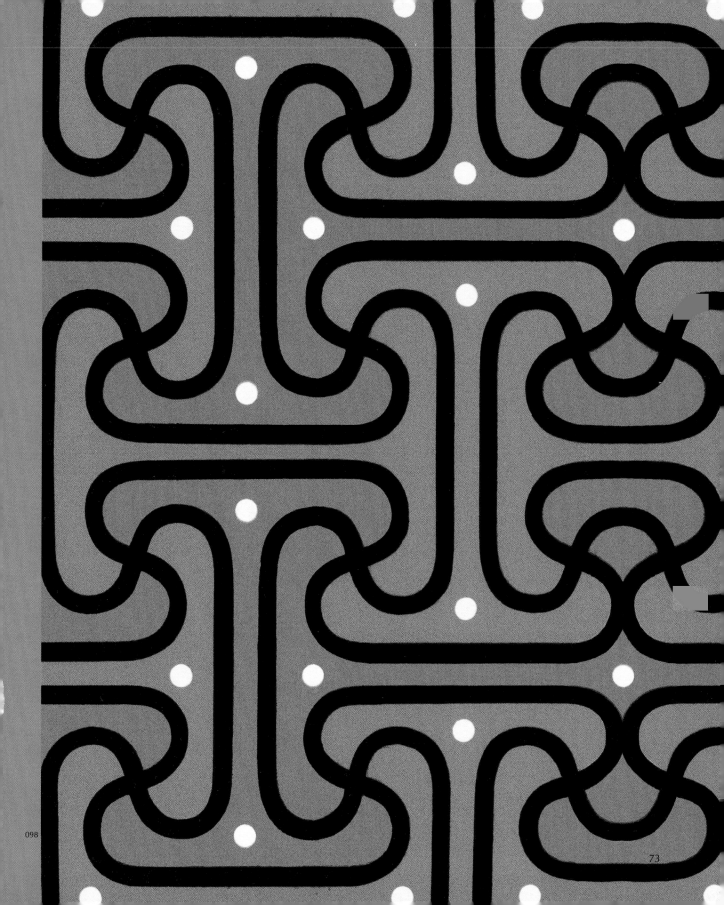

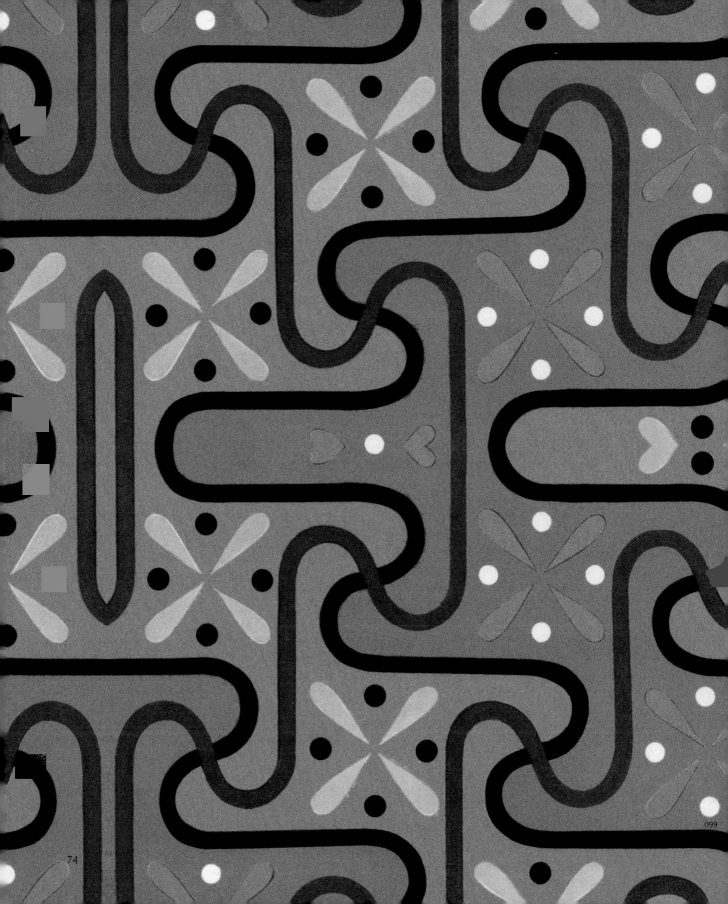

100

101

102

103

104 (background)

80

107

108

109

110

111

112

113

114

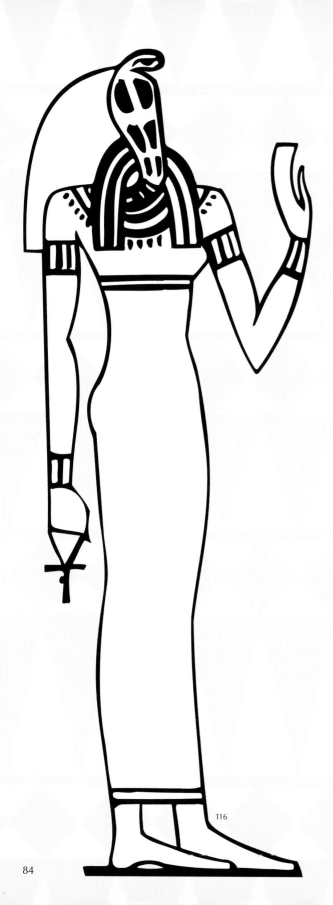

116

118

119   120

121

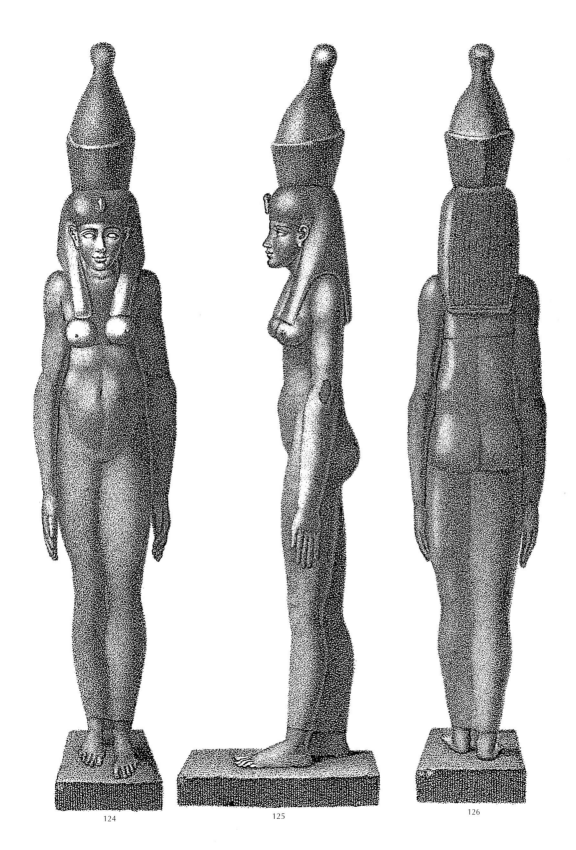

124   125   126

127

128

131

132

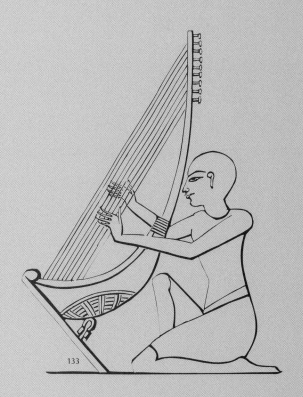

133

134

137

138

139

140 141

99

142

143

100

144

145

146

147 148

149

151 150

152 153

154

102 155 156

158

159

160

161

162

163

164

157

165

159

103

166

167

169

168

104

170

171

172

173

174

175

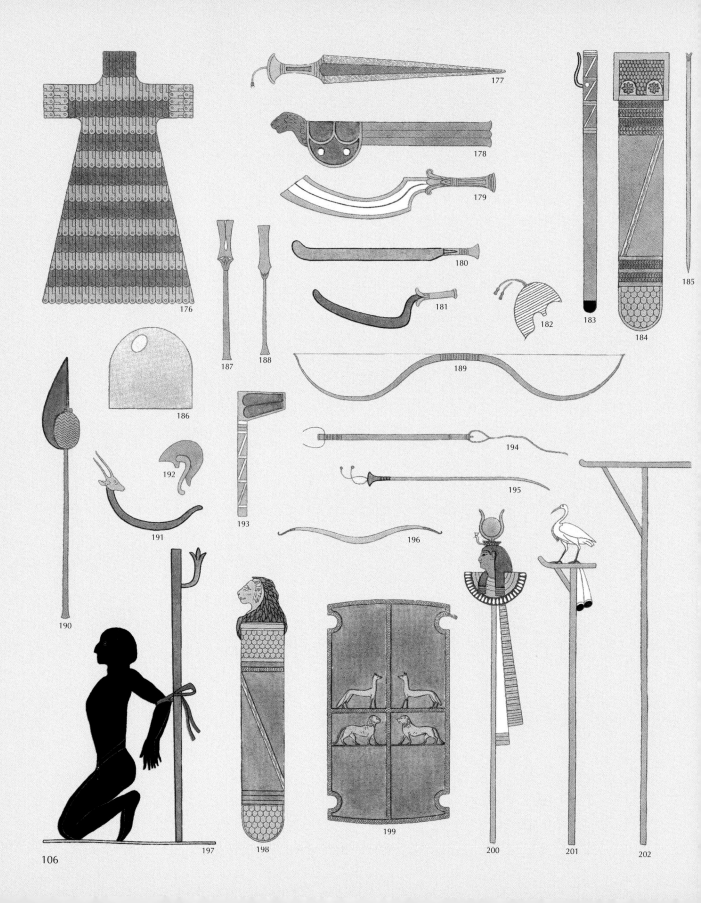

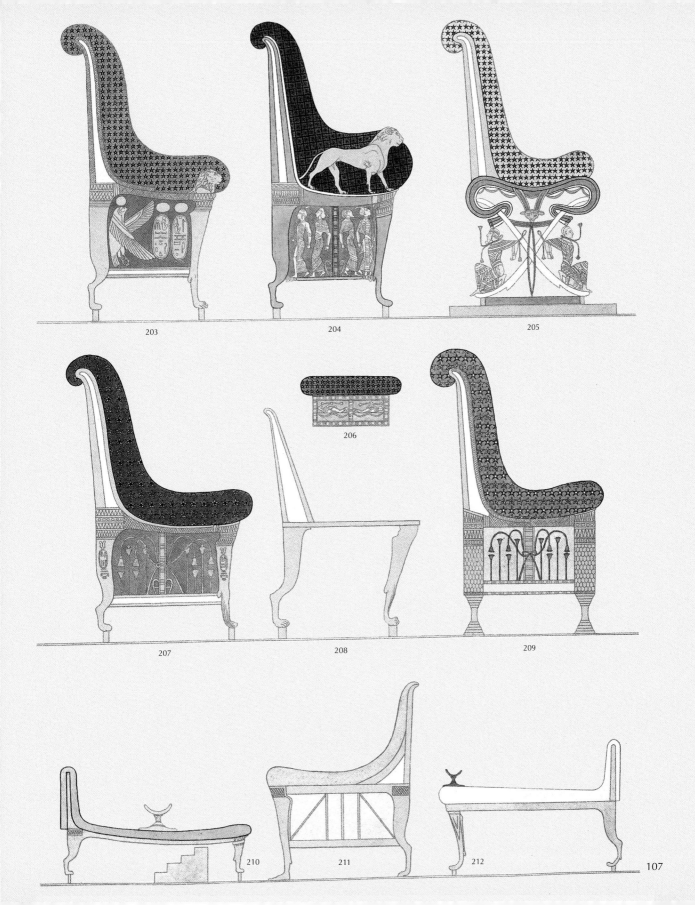

203   204   205

206

207   208   209

210   211   212   107

213

214

215   216   217   218   219   220   221   222   223   224   225   226   227   228

229

230

231

232

233

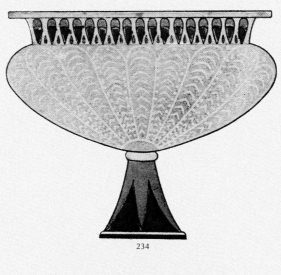

234

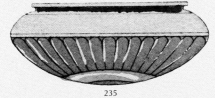

235

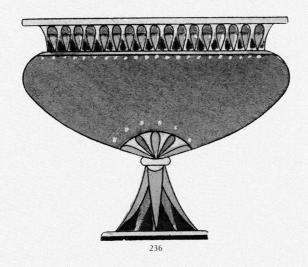

236

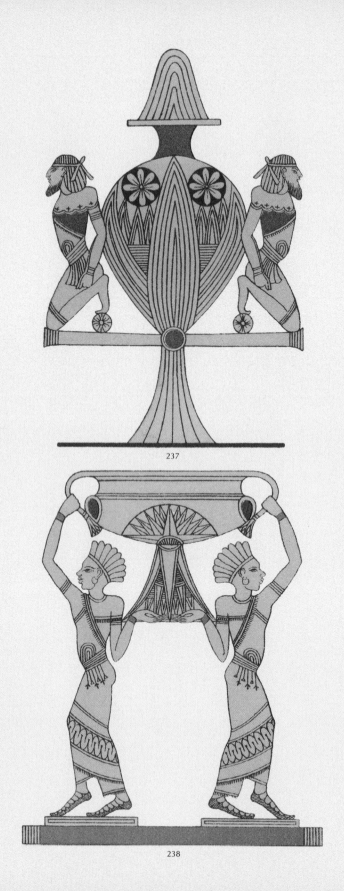

237

238

239

240

242

243

244

245

246

247

248

249

250

251

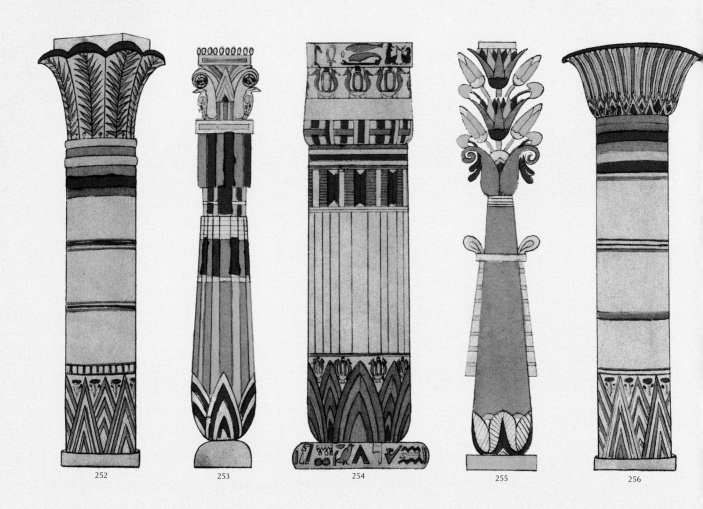

252 253 254 255 256

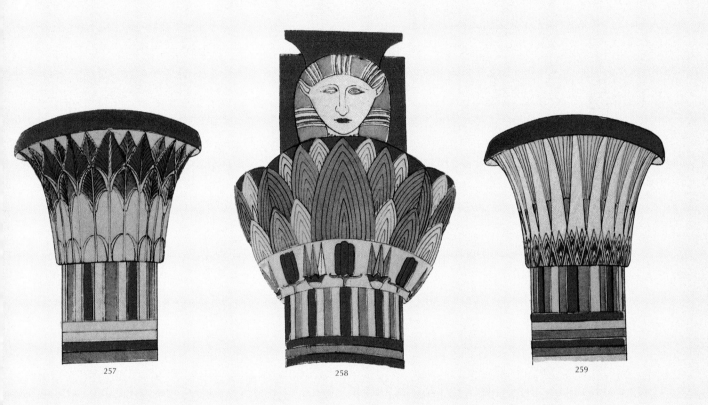

257   258   259

119

260

261

262

263

264

265

266

267

268

270

271

272

273

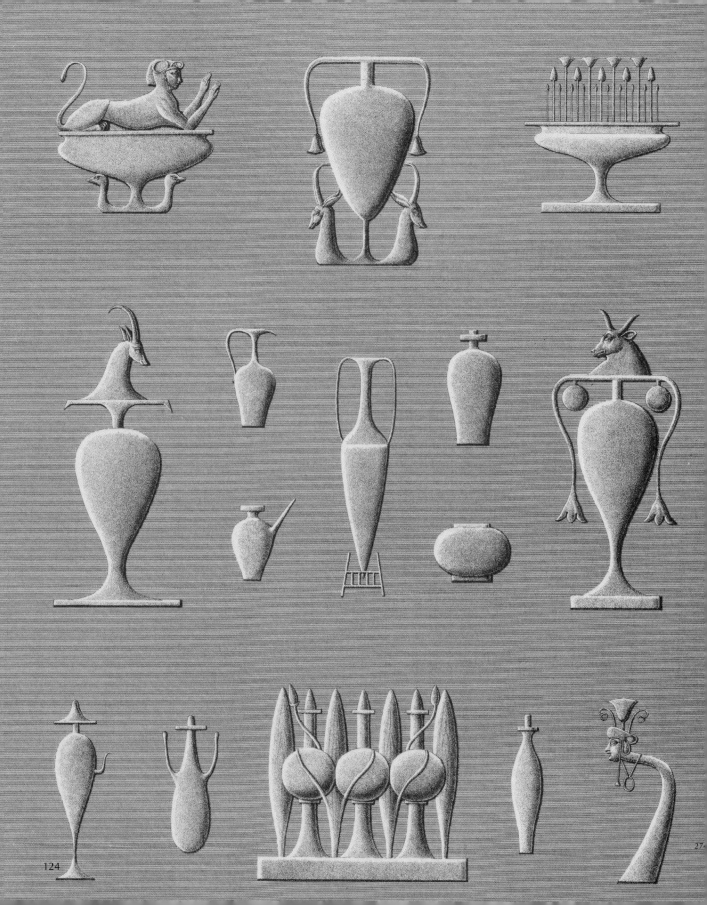

275

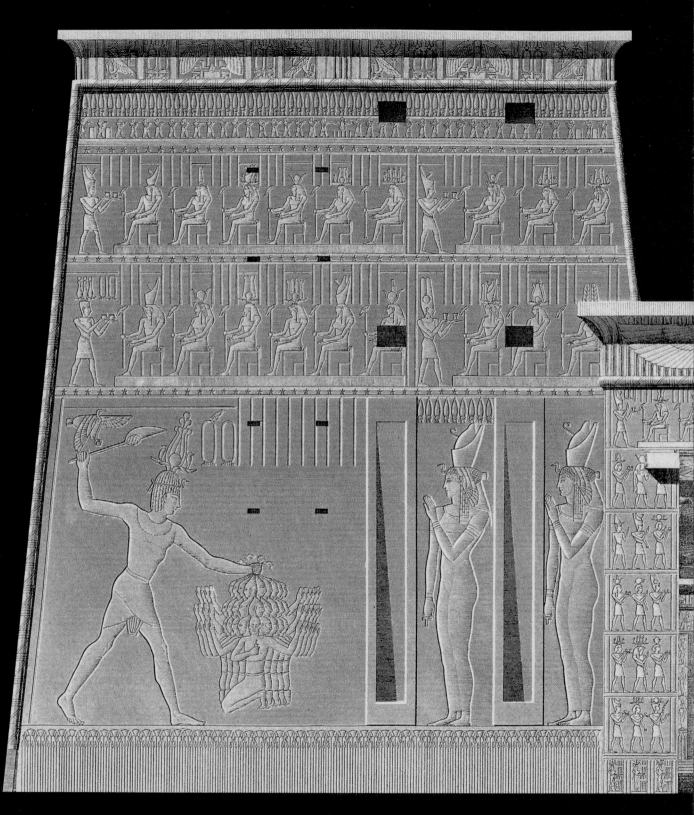